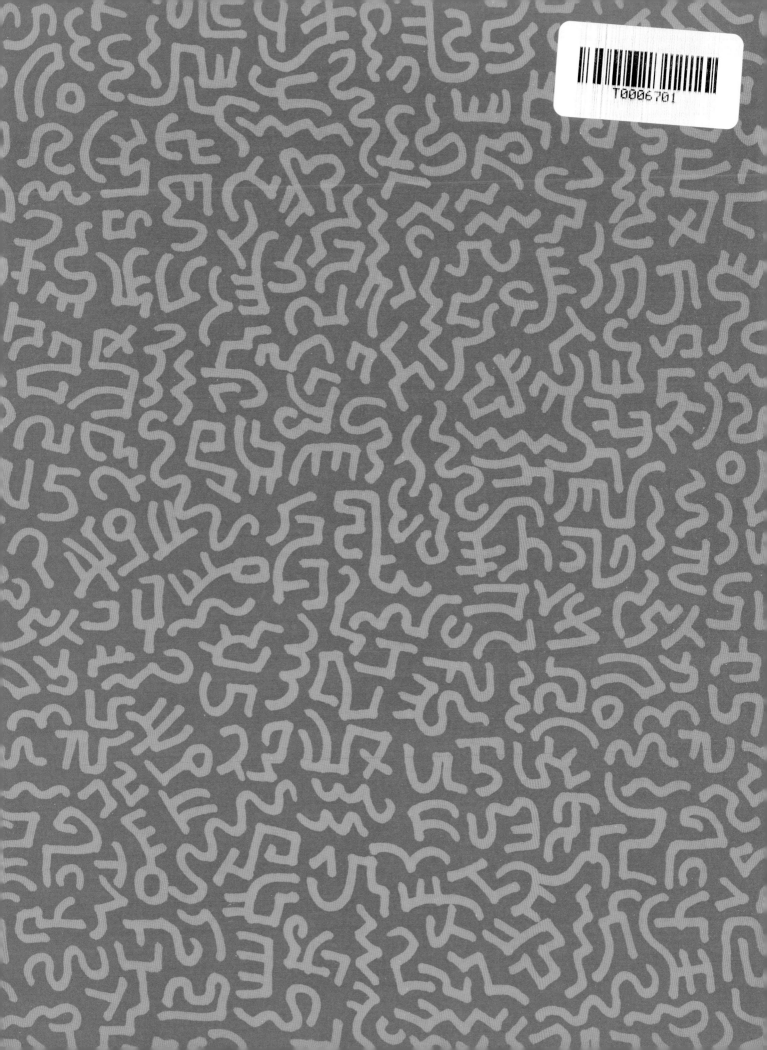

T0006701

For Will
—T.L.B.

For Karen
—K.N.

Farrar Straus Giroux Books for Young Readers
An imprint of Macmillan Publishing Group, LLC
120 Broadway, New York, NY 10271

Text copyright © 2020 by Tami Lewis Brown
Illustrations copyright © 2020 by Keith Negley
All rights reserved
Color separations by Bright Arts (H.K.) Ltd.
Printed in China by Hung Hing Off-set Printing Co. Ltd.,
Heshan City, Guangdong Province
Art directed by Jen Keenan
Designed by Andrea Sparacio
First edition, 2020

1 3 5 7 9 10 8 6 4 2

mackids.com

Library of Congress Control Number: 2020904482

Our books may be purchased in bulk for promotional, educational, or business use.
Please contact your local bookseller or the Macmillan Corporate and Premium Sales Department
at (800) 221-7945 ext. 5442 or by email at MacmillanSpecialMarkets@macmillan.com.

Art Is Life

THE LIFE OF ARTIST KEITH HARING

WORDS BY
TAMI LEWIS BROWN

PICTURES BY
KEITH NEGLEY

Farrar Straus Giroux
New York

When Keith Haring was a small boy in a small town in Pennsylvania, he sat on his father's lap, doodling dragons and dogs, circles and snakes.

He shut his eyes and drew fast and sure, scribbling and scrawling yellow and green imaginary things that only he could see.

"When I grow up, I would like to be an artist," Keith wrote when he was ten. "The reason is because I like to draw."

So nearly every minute of every day, Keith drew.

Art flowed from his fingers, and it welled up inside him, in his heart and his imagination.

Everywhere Keith went, it was as if art was all around him.

ART was Keith's **LIFE**,

and his **LIFE** was **ART**.

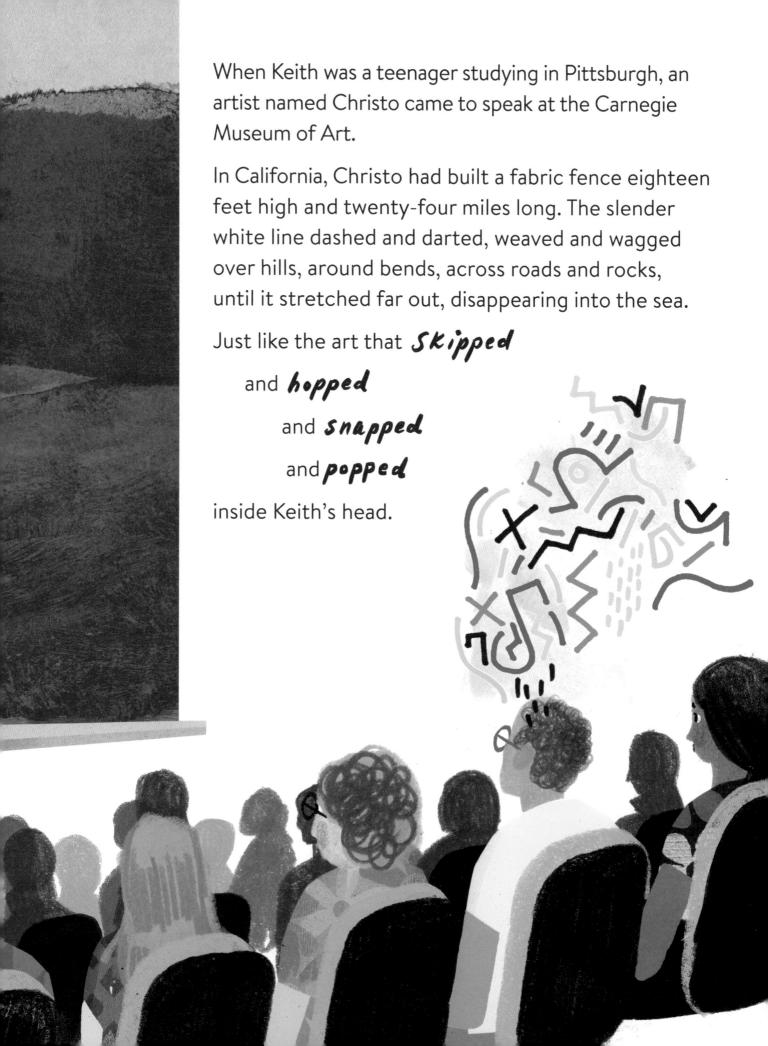

When Keith was a teenager studying in Pittsburgh, an artist named Christo came to speak at the Carnegie Museum of Art.

In California, Christo had built a fabric fence eighteen feet high and twenty-four miles long. The slender white line dashed and darted, weaved and wagged over hills, around bends, across roads and rocks, until it stretched far out, disappearing into the sea.

Just like the art that *skipped*

and *hopped*

and *snapped*

and *popped*

inside Keith's head.

At first, some people didn't like Christo's art.
But once they saw the dancing river of cloth,
they began to understand something new

about **art**

and about **beauty**

and about the **world** we live in.

As Keith watched Christo's film and heard him speak, he understood, too.

"The public needs art," he wrote in his journal.

"Art is for everybody.

ART IS LIFE. LIFE IS ART."

When Keith was twenty, he attended the School of Visual Arts—in New York. He taped long strips of paper over the classroom walls, and rolled even more across the floor.

With a brush and a pot of paint, he *swooped*

and he *swung*

   he *lined*

      and he *striped*.

Black paint splashed as the thick brush dashed, swiping patterns to the beat of loud, thumping music—the way his father had taught him when he was small—

until finally the whole room was covered with the strange shapes that rumbled inside Keith's brain.

And Keith was left
with art all around him.

As much as the teachers and students and everybody else loved Keith's lively art, they loved Keith—his enthusiasm and exuberance, his joy and jubilance—even more.

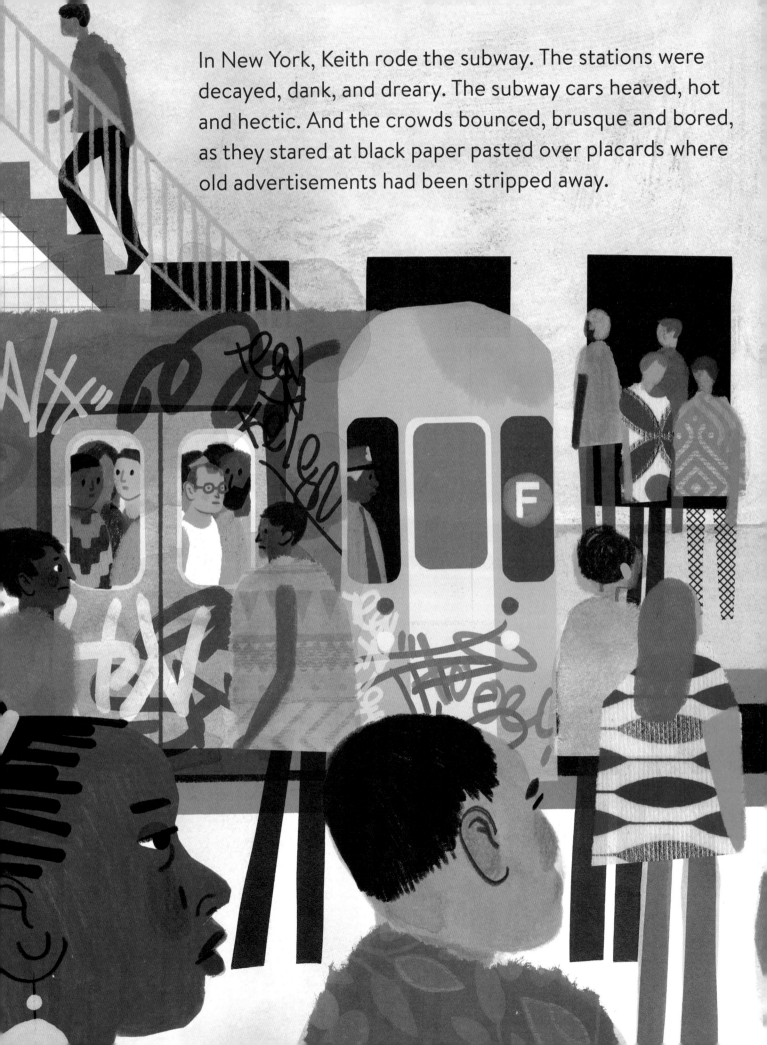

In New York, Keith rode the subway. The stations were decayed, dank, and dreary. The subway cars heaved, hot and hectic. And the crowds bounced, brusque and bored, as they stared at black paper pasted over placards where old advertisements had been stripped away.

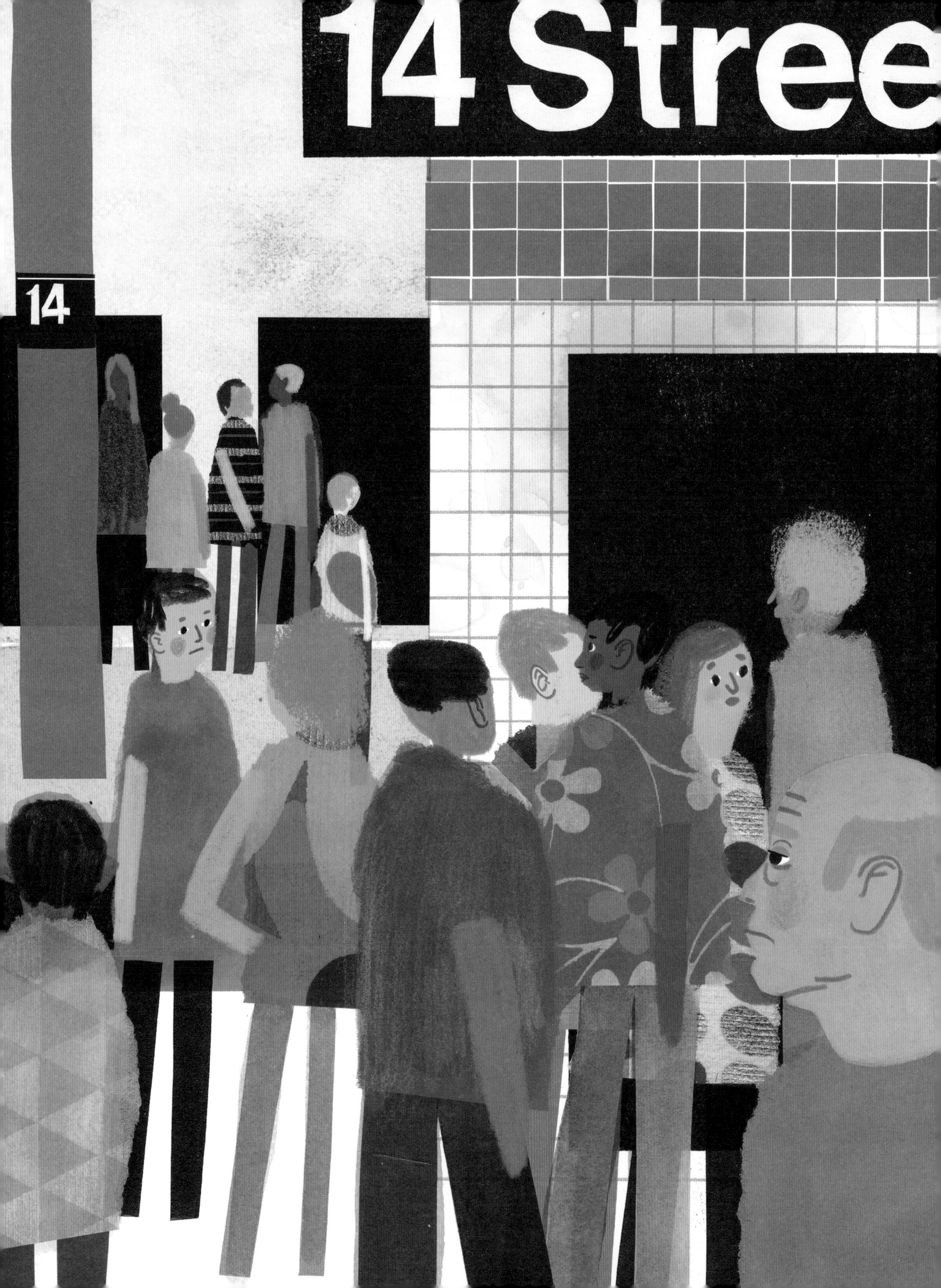
14 Stree
14

Keith knew that the streets and the subways and the people of New York needed art all around them, too.

Art that could make their imaginations dance and prance, roar and soar, just like the art inside Keith's head.

So one day, just a bit more than a year after he'd arrived in the city, Keith had an artful idea.

He ran up the subway station stairs to the
street and he bought a stick of white chalk.

ART IS LIFE, he thought to himself

Then he marched back down into the subway station.

Chalk dust swirled as Keith's art unfurled where everyone could see it.

Ringed with rays of light and energy, radiant babies crawled.
Washed with waves of sound and commotion, joyful dogs barked.

Stunned by sketches of dancing men and spaceships and robots and dollar bills, surprised commuters stopped and stared . . .

And some of them began
to *imagine*
and **understand**
and *laugh*
and **Cheer**
and **clap** their hands.

Police stopped him—and sometimes even arrested him—for drawing on the walls. Sometimes Keith was scared, for himself and for other young artists whose work came under attack.

But . . . "Sometimes I finish," he said,
"and there's applause from the whole station."

There were people who thought his pictures were just scribbles. They said he was making a mess.

Others thought his pictures were gorgeous.
They believed he was making masterpieces.

Before long, Keith was invited to
hang his pictures in art galleries,

but he would keep sneaking
them onto alley walls, too.

He painted boisterous crowds hugging or cheering or working together. He built massive sculptures that filled park lawns and tiny ones that fit on shelves.

He drew winged angels and a man with three eyes and dancing cats and throbbing hearts.

ART IS LIFE. LIFE IS ART,

he remembered.

Almost overnight it seemed, Keith and his radiant babies and barking dogs and zapping robots and all the rest of his creations were famous. But he still wanted everyone to see and feel art all around them.

In 1986, he opened a store in the SoHo neighborhood of New York City, and called it the Pop Shop.

He made pictures against racism and drug abuse, pictures supporting unity and love, and toys and T-shirts, posters and pens—inexpensive art anyone could take home. He welcomed everyone to come and see, and even to buy: kids from the Bronx who spray-painted graffiti, and ladies from Park Avenue, who were draped in minks and pearls.

Down the streets, Keith's art
popped on shirts and sneakers.

On museum walls, Keith's dogs barked at
Monet's water lilies and Picasso's acrobats.

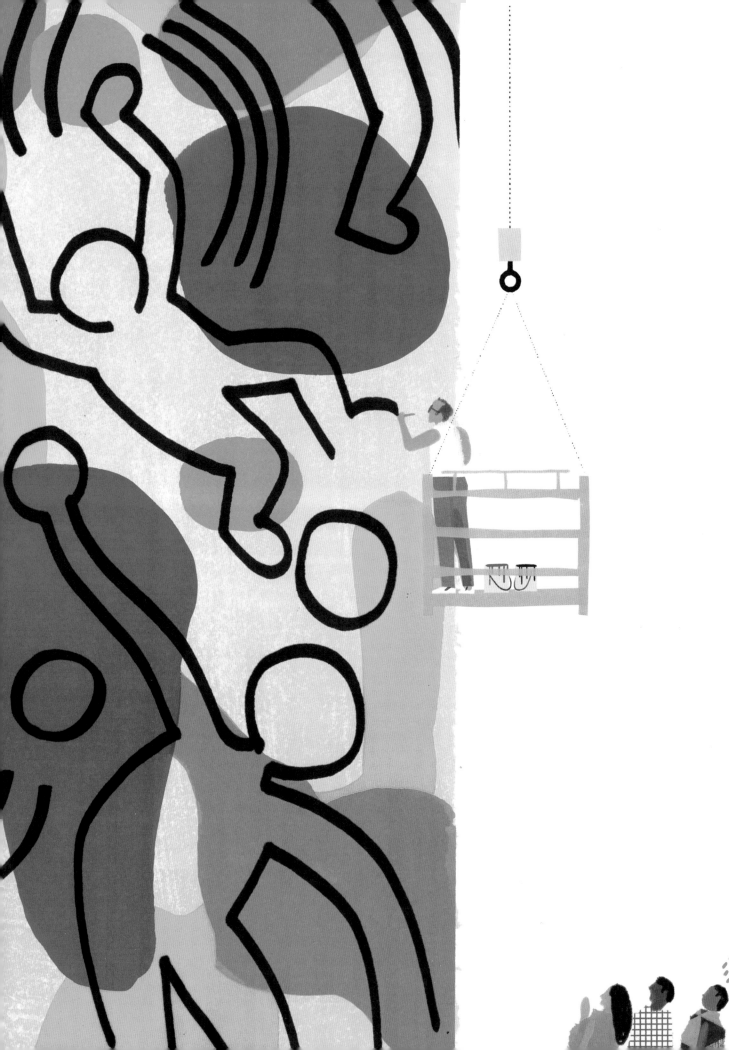

From New York to California, Tokyo to Paris, Keith painted everywhere—for everyone.

Some of his artwork made grown-ups blush. Others made children laugh and old people smile.

Most of all, Keith's art made people dream
and *imagine*
and *think*
and **understand** a little more than they had before
about *art*
and *life*
and the world we live in.

Keith Haring died in February 1990, when he was just thirty-one years old, but his art still surrounds us today—pictures that make people *smile* and *laugh* and *cry* and *think*, drawings that *buzz* and *whir* and *shout* and *whisper*,

paintings that look simple but help us understand complicated ideas, art that *inspires* and *inquires* and **opens** imaginations—like Keith Haring, the artist whose

LIFE WAS A WORK OF ART.

AUTHOR'S NOTE

KEITH HARING was born on May 4, 1958, and lived with his mom, dad, and three younger sisters in Kutztown, Pennsylvania, a small town about seventy miles north of Philadelphia. Keith's father drew cartoons for fun, and he and Keith sometimes communicated in Morse code.

As a young man, Keith studied commercial art, but right away he knew that drawing advertisements and logos was not for him. He traveled across the country following a band named the Grateful Dead and trying to find his own path. In 1978, his father drove him from Pennsylvania to New York City to attend the School of Visual Arts and become a "real" artist. Keith studied painting and semiotics (symbols) and experimented with video, a new art medium in those days. Soon he was known throughout the school for his enthusiasm, kindness, and near-constant art making.

New York's East Village, where Keith lived, was a vibrant, edgy neighborhood filled with artists, musicians, actors, and ordinary people. One night, Keith met a young musician named Madonna playing at a small club near his apartment and they became lifelong friends. Subway artist Jean-Michel Basquiat, another superstar-to-be, was a close friend, too.

During his early months in New York, Keith created art shows and performances all over the neighborhood—and he rode the subway to a part-time job picking wildflowers from traffic medians and selling them to florists.

Keith's subway drawings instantly attracted widespread attention. Well-known art dealers asked if they could show his work, and art icon Andy Warhol invited him for tea. Andy and Keith were good friends from that moment on.

By early 1982, newspaper and television reports were buzzing about a man who drew art for everybody, and Keith had achieved his childhood dream of being an artist. "In one year my art has taken me to Europe and propelled me into a kind of limelight," he wrote in his diary. He was invited to paint murals, erect statues, and show his art all over the world. He even painted a mural about unity and peace on the Berlin Wall, which at that time divided free West Berlin from Communist-controlled East Berlin.

Keith Haring loved to create art with kids because he admired children's honesty, courage, and ability to say exactly what they felt—the same qualities he sought to convey in his own work. His art was, at its core, his way of communicating, and he believed children were his most important audience. He said, "In a way, it's as important to communicate to one person, one ten-year-old person, as it is to try to make any kind of big effect on the entire world."

In 1986, he worked with nine hundred children in New York City to paint a banner celebrating the Statue of Liberty's one hundredth birthday, and he wrote (and illustrated, of course) a wonderful book for children called *Nina's Book of Little Things*. In 2008, a forty-eight-foot-tall balloon inspired by Keith's *Man with a Heart* debuted in the Macy's Thanksgiving Day Parade.

In 1987, Keith was diagnosed with AIDS. Although he received the best medical care available, at the time there were no drugs that could halt the disease. Even as his health grew worse, Keith continued to make art for everybody all over the world and worked hard to spread the word about AIDS prevention. Just hours before he died, on February 16, 1990, he asked for a pencil and paper and slowly scrawled the figure of a radiant baby. He was only thirty-one years old.

ILLUSTRATOR'S NOTE

I WAS ECSTATIC when I got the call to work on a picture-book biography of Keith Haring. When deciding where to get my MFA, it was the School of Visual Arts in New York City that I picked, partly because I knew legends like Keith Haring studied there. To be able to walk some of the same halls and streets he had was truly inspiring for me. However, how do you draw a book meant to showcase someone's art without actually showing their art? This was harder than I had realized when I agreed to do the book. It was important to me that readers came away feeling familiar with his work, but it was a challenge finding the right balance of my art looking just enough like his, without actually *being* his. It wasn't until I stopped forcing it that I hit the balance I had been aiming for. I instead focused on depicting the energy that Haring created and imagined it as three-dimensional shapes flowing in and around crowds of people. Focusing on showing the energy and enthusiasm he had was the key to tackling the art; everything fell in line after that. It was also important for me to make reference to Keith Haring's relentless pursuit of AIDS awareness. The endpapers of this book are left unfinished—inspired by his final painting, *Unfinished Painting*, 1989, made to look incomplete intentionally. It represents his feelings about AIDS, the many people who would be taken by the disease, and the lack of government funding. I think it's one of his most poignant pieces, since he knew he wasn't long for this world and that he would never see the life he had planned for himself completed.

KID-FRIENDLY RESOURCES ON KEITH AND RELATED ARTISTS

The Keith Haring Foundation website, HaringKids.com, has games, activities, art projects, lesson plans, and more. Read more about Keith in:

Haring, Kay. *Keith Haring: The Boy Who Just Kept Drawing.* Illustrated by Robert Neubecker. New York: Dial, 2017.

Keith was influenced by his good friends, artists Andy Warhol and Jean-Michel Basquiat. Read more about Andy and Jean-Michel in these books:

Steptoe, Javaka. *Radiant Child: The Story of Young Artist Jean-Michel Basquiat.* New York: Little Brown BFYR, 2016.

Christensen, Bonnie. *Fabulous: A Portrait of Andy Warhol.* New York: Henry Holt, 2011.

Warhola, James. *Uncle Andy's: A Faabbbulous Visit with Andy.* New York: Putnam, 2003.

**In 1990, shortly before he died, a French reporter asked Keith which other artist he'd like to be, and Keith immediately answered, "Pablo Picasso."
Learn about Picasso as a boy:**

Winter, Jonah. *Just Behave, Pablo Picasso!* Illustrated by Kevin Hawkes. New York: Arthur A. Levine, 2012.

RESOURCES FOR ADULTS

Books:

Deitch, Jeffrey, Suzanne Geiss, and Julia Gruen. *Keith Haring.* New York: Rizzoli, 2014.

Gruen, John. *Keith Haring: The Authorized Biography.* New York: Simon & Schuster, 1991.

Haring, Keith. *Keith Haring Journals.* New York: Penguin, 2010.

Films:

Aubert, Elisabeth, Gina Belafonte, Keith Haring, Dennis Hopper, and Barbara Haskell. *Drawing the Line: A Portrait of Keith Haring.* West Long Branch, NJ: Biografilm Associates, 1989.

Clausen, Christina, et al. *The Universe of Keith Haring.* New York: Arthouse Films, 2010.

Maysles, David, Charlotte Zwerin, and Albert Maysles. *Running Fence.* New York: Maysles Films, 1977.

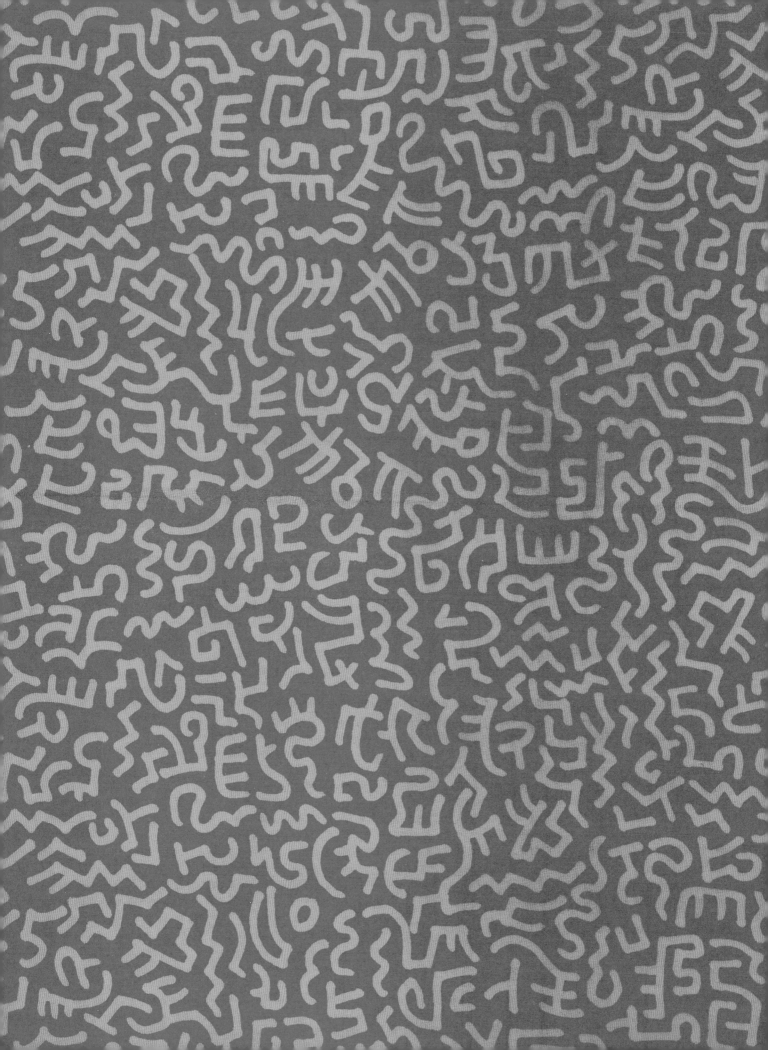